the birth date book

This Book Belongs to

Lindsey Nash

The Birth Date Book

July 1

What Your Birth Date Reveals about You

Marietta Benevento

Illustrated by Claude Martinot

Ariel Books

Andrews McMeel Publishing

Kansas City

www.andrewsmcmeel.com

ISBN: 0-8362-6140-2

Series editor: Sue Carnahan
Series design by Junie Lee
Typesetting by Nina Gaskin

CONTENTS

introduction

Your birth date is more than just a passing squiggle on the calendar, more than an excuse to exceed your daily calorie ration. Your birth date is a *fate*ful day; a day where the forces of the universe came together in a unique way to chart your destiny; a moment in time imprinted on your very being. Who you are, where you've been, where you're headed—all of these things had their beginning on the month, day, and hour of your birth.

The Birth Date Book sheds some light

on these influences and offers a series of snapshots of who you are. Are you glamorous and outgoing like Cindy Crawford, coolly buttoned-down like Sidney Poitier, or an unpredictable mixture of the two? Why do you prefer a particular color, taste, or scent? What career paths appeal to you? Do you harbor a secret vocation in esoteric anthropology, or does crunching numbers send you into paroxysms of joy? What about your home? Is it styled with the spacious calm of a

Zen monastery or riotously festooned like a Jamaican nightclub? Who can inspire you to drop everything and go to the ends of the earth? And who sends you running lickety-split for the nearest exit?

You'll find both surprising *and* familiar answers to these questions in the following pages. Consider this book a toast to your special day—and to the exceptional being that you are now, and continue to become every day of your life.

your astrological

sun sign

CANCER

Cancer, the Crab, is perhaps the most sensitive—and definitely the moodiest—sign in the zodiac. So it's no surprise that the word "crabby" is often associated with this sign. Like the crab, whose hard shell protects a vulnerable and defenseless body, those born under the sign of Cancer feel the need to defend themselves from the assaults of everyday life. You are easily crushed by a harsh word or a cold stare. Although Cancers require special handling, they respond with warmth, tenderness, and kindness.

Also known as Moon Children, Cancers are often described as dreamy and impressionable. You are wholeheartedly devoted to mother, family, food, and home. In fact, a comfortable environment, brimming with love and security, is crucial.

You tend to collect possessions (including cash) because, like the crab, once something is in your grip, you just can't let it go. Often misinterpreted as clinginess, this propensity for deep attachment is actually a cosmic necessity for Cancers!

You are highly introspective and wise beyond your years. Cancers are known to be the most psychic sign in the zodiac, and others will frequently turn to you for advice, support, and tenderness. You do brood at times, often becoming self-indulgent and lazy, but most Cancers conscientiously keep the home fires burning and radiate warmth to the whole zodiac.

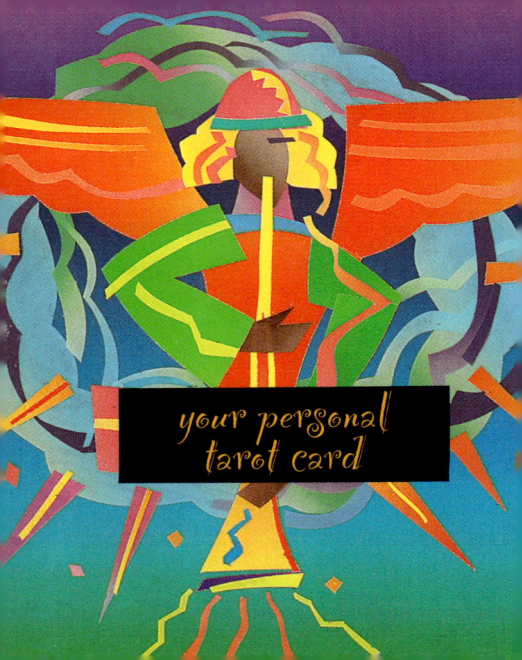

your personal
tarot card

JUDGMENT

Judgment is the twentieth card of the Major Arcana, the twenty-two most powerful cards in the tarot deck. Judgment represents your ability to free yourself from a difficult situation or relationship by committing to a decision and taking action. Embrace changes and endings as new chances to learn and grow . . . and as an excuse to indulge in ice cream while you cope with the transition!

your chinese
astrological symbol

Your sign comes around only once every twelve years in the Chinese zodiac, but during that year your number will definitely come up a winner in the cosmic lottery. Each sign is governed by the qualities of a particular animal guardian. Are you patient as an ox? Wise as a snake? Vain as a monkey? Locate the year of your birth in the chart below to find out— if you dare.

THE YEAR OF THE RAT

1900, 1912, 1924, 1936,
1948, 1960, 1972, 1984, 1996

Popular, ambitious, honest, and stubborn

THE YEAR OF THE OX

1901, 1913, 1925, 1937,
1949, 1961, 1973, 1985,
1997

Patient, strong, original, and rigid

THE YEAR OF THE TIGER

1902, 1914, 1926, 1938,
1950, 1962, 1974, 1986, 1998

Generous, noble, passionate, and hotheaded

THE YEAR OF THE RABBIT

1903, 1915, 1927, 1939,
1951, 1963, 1975, 1987,
1999

Discreet, sensitive, clever, and devious

THE YEAR OF THE DRAGON

1904, 1916, 1928, 1940, 1952, 1964, 1976, 1988, 2000
Enthusiastic, intuitive, shrewd, and demanding

THE YEAR OF THE SNAKE

1905, 1917, 1929, 1941, 1953, 1965, 1977, 1989, 2001
Wise, compassionate, elegant, and extravagant

THE YEAR OF THE HORSE

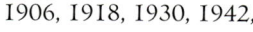

1906, 1918, 1930, 1942, 1954, 1966, 1978, 1990, 2002

Independent, hardworking, charming, and rebellious

THE YEAR OF THE GOAT

1907, 1919, 1931, 1943, 1955, 1967, 1979, 1991, 2003

Creative, tasteful, lovable, and fickle

THE YEAR OF THE MONKEY

1908, 1920, 1932, 1944, 1956, 1968, 1980, 1992, 2004

Witty, nimble, passionate, and vain

THE YEAR OF THE ROOSTER

1909, 1921, 1933, 1945, 1957, 1969, 1981, 1993, 2005

Frank, talented, industrious, and pompous

THE YEAR OF THE DOG

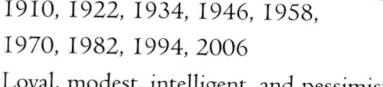

1910, 1922, 1934, 1946, 1958, 1970, 1982, 1994, 2006

Loyal, modest, intelligent, and pessimistic

THE YEAR OF THE PIG

1911, 1923, 1935, 1947, 1959, 1971, 1983, 1995, 2007

Honest, sociable, cultured, and gullible

crowning jewel

RUBY

Rubies vary in color from a pale red to a deep purple known as "pigeon blood." Flawless ones are extremely rare. They have been used throughout history to inspire courage and energy and to protect against destruction and cruelty. Considered the truly royal stone, rubies are esteemed for their transparent brilliance. Those who wear them, however, are admired for their impeccable taste!

lucky number

TWENTY

Twenty is the number of rebirth—and you are always reborn into better circumstances! Your personality is constantly evolving, enriching you with experiences both broad and profound, and you possess the curiosity and wisdom to enjoy them. You also maintain an inspiring brightness because of your unquenchable, childlike enthusiasm—a benefit of your moment-by-moment renewal!

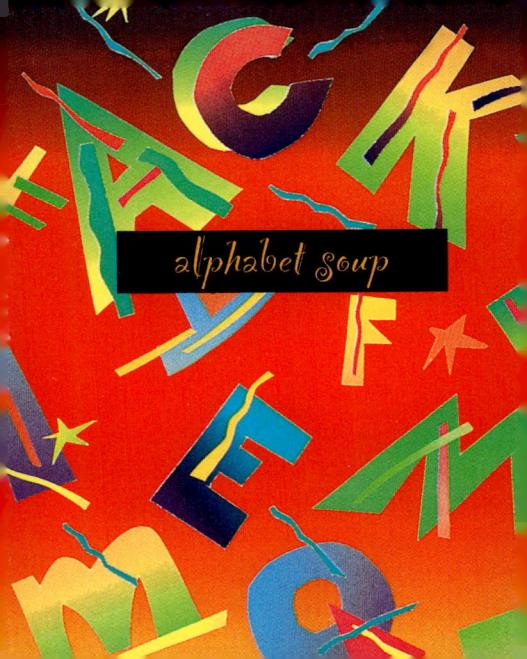

alphabet soup

E, C, and S

July 1's often find that names and places beginning with the following letters become especially significant during the course of their lives: *E, C,* and *S*. For a charismatic person like you, *empathy* and *charm* will put you in the right place at the right time. But *secrecy* is an important part of your attraction, so don't unfold your mysteries too quickly!

week link

FRIDAY

Friday is mystically associated with Venus, the planet of love, romance, and personal growth. This lucky connection brings both passion and harmony into your life. Luxuriate in your intriguing Venusian pastimes—a playful flirtation or an artistic project that starts your creativity flowing. Friday is the day to revel in your passions and enjoy your true nature!

your magical food

BANANAS

There must be people who don't like bananas, but they are very rare. You are almost universally well liked. July 1's always seem simple, kind, and uncomplicated because they most often *are* simple, kind, and uncomplicated. You're confident, too, without a trace of arrogance. No need for you to play Top Banana; you already know who you are!

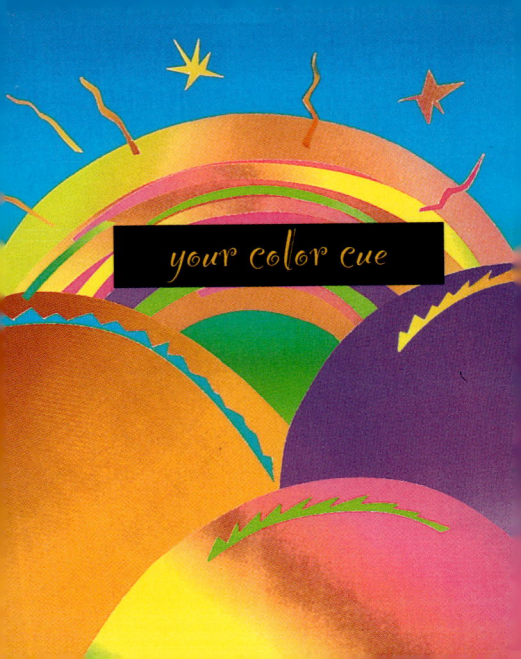

your color cue

MIDNIGHT BLUE

For you, nighttime can be the right time. Most July 1's are just coming alive at the bewitching hour (if you're not, you often wish you could be!). Sometimes sly, often secretive, and always intriguing, you are most at ease on the cusp of night. Blue is the color of the spirit, midnight the hour of the soul. No other color could ever enfold you so completely.

flower power

TULIPS

Tulips, the harbingers of springtime, announce their arrival in a riot of color. July 1's often make the same kind of entrance. Bold, exuberant, and aggressive, your presence cannot be ignored. But no one wants to ignore you anyway! Your unbridled enthusiasm is welcome—and contagious. Though few can match your energy, many happily (and hopefully) give it a try.

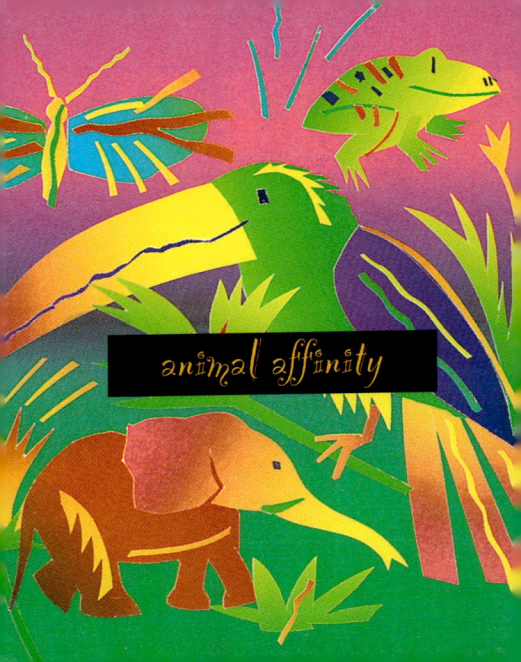

animal affinity

DOG

Faithful friend and confidant, the dog has stood by its human companion ever since the first fire was lit in a prehistoric cave. In a similar manner, July Is' bonds are strong, and their loyalty is legendary. But thanks to your playful spirit, you carry your deeply committed nature with the grace of a Cary Grant, effortlessly bringing joy and happiness to everyone in your extended "pack"!

your first desire

COMFORT

More than anything else, July 1's tend to seek comfort in life—in their wardrobes, home decor, relationships, work environments, and social situations. When you feel outwardly comfortable, it helps boost your inner confidence and allows your *best* self to shine through.

your secret wish

On the surface, most July 1's live quietly. Underneath, however, you hope to make a dramatic difference! Whether that means changing even one other person's life for the better or contributing something positive to the world at large, it really doesn't matter. Knowing that you helped is enough . . . although a *little* public recognition wouldn't necessarily be so bad!

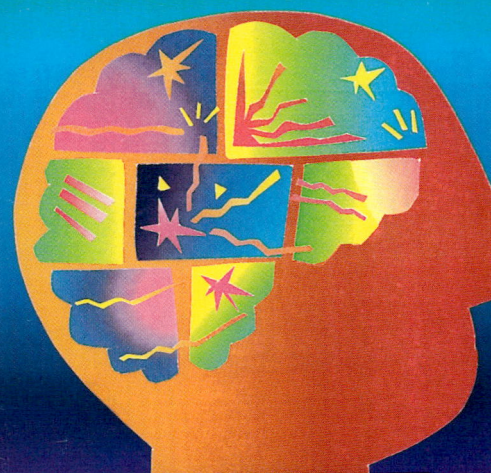

personality profile

July I's are multifaceted and multi-talented and generally a pleasure to be around. Chances are that you're also trying very hard to become a multi-millionaire!

At the core, July I's are steady, consistent, and dependable—but on the surface, they can seem somewhat unpredictable! You may be quiet and pensive one minute, then blabbering away the next. Or you can spend weeks nesting at home, then suddenly go out and do the town night after night!

Your changing July 1 moods can leave your wide circle of friends and acquaintances asking, "What's next?" For the most part, July 1's are upbeat and positive, but every now and then they can get mired in the deepest funks, sometimes without apparent cause.

This moodiness doesn't mean you'll sing the blues for all to hear, however, because you are apt to be somewhat secretive. You'll only rarely cry on someone else's shoulder, even though you're among the first to lend a sympathetic ear. This independence can be admirable, but sometimes maybe you *need* to accept others' help.

Most July 1's are deeply affected by music and the arts. Your tastes may run the gamut from punk to classical, and you might value everything from Michelangelo to modern abstract, or from rock to Bach! A dimly lit little dive of a jazz club could be your idea of paradise, and a trendy new furniture gallery might tickle your fancy—and threaten your pocketbook!—for months.

At the same time, July 1's are usually careful with money and slow to splurge on frivolous, vain, or unnecessary expenses. That new sports car may look sleek and breezy, but who needs it, when your old station wagon still gets you where you want to go? And yet that fabulous player piano may sing to your soul . . . !

It's not uncommon for July 1's to have multiple stashes of cash hidden around the house—anywhere from the cookie jar to the toe of a shoe! You might also make it your business to know how to diversify your assets with stocks, bonds, or mutual funds. Your many moods even affect the different ways you put your money to work for you!

But regardless of how you invest your money, you'll still spend enough to make yourself and those you care for amply comfortable. Clever July 1's typically still have something put aside for a rainy day!

room for improvement

July 1s' tendencies to display a quick-changing array of temperamental reactions may cause others to see them as inconsistent and unpredictable. There's nothing wrong with voicing your feelings, but it might be a good idea to keep *some* of your knee-jerk responses to yourself. Try taking the time to let your head or heart cool before blurting out a too-hasty retort.

If one of your gloomier moods descends, be careful not to wallow in the misery or else it might start to feel as comfortable as a warm bath. Once July I's settle into the habit of feeling low, rising up out of that soggy routine can often be a little challenging!

Be equally careful that love for good home cooking and a taste for fine dining don't gang up on you! Comfort foods can be soothing, but they're often high in calories as well. Rigorous exercise isn't usually a July I strong suit, so do watch out for those extra ounces and pounds that can all too quickly appear. Remember, you want to be comfortable with what you see in the mirror!

Because July 1's are inclined to be secretive, they may feel overwhelmed at times by accumulated worries and fears. You might need to open up and pour out your heart to someone else now and then. Whether it's one-on-one counseling or simply confiding in a friend, sharing your innermost thoughts could lift a considerable burden from your strong yet sensitive shoulders!

on the job

July 1's have multiple interests and talents that could be put to use in a variety of financially and personally rewarding careers.

Your ability to keep your eye on the bottom line might make you an excellent accountant, a crackerjack construction estimator, or a powerful CEO! For more latitude, being a merchandise buyer would let you use your financial skills, indulge your love of travel, and use your keen eye for spotting the latest trends!

Enthusiasm for cooking, fine dining,

and food in general may draw many July 1's to the restaurant industry. You might be deliciously happy behind the stove as a chef or out front managing the floor for the hottest new restaurant in town. And having your own catering business might be exactly your "dish"!

Many July 1's are interested in history and can grow very nostalgic about the past, so a position with a museum, historical society, or landmarks preservation committee could offer the sort of work they would treasure.

Running an art or photography gallery would bring July Is' considerable talent-search skills into the career picture. In addition, you'd probably be the one to pick the background music (perhaps from your own vast collection) to set *just* the right mood for each show!

Whatever career path you follow, try to make your working environment as comfortable as possible. Clean, well-lighted, and spacious work areas can do *wonders* for July Is' productivity!

at play

At work, July I's can be serious and industrious, always keeping that nose stuck firmly to the grindstone. Come playtime, however, you'll rarely sniff at a chance to have fun!

Typical July I's are apt to be up for a full-tilt party. Having a good time is high on your list of priorities, and you are willing to seek out pleasure wherever you can.

Your interest in history makes travel a pastime you will probably indulge whenever you get such an opportunity. Ambling across ancient ruins in the hills of New Mexico, for example, or viewing the masterpieces in the Louvre would be ideal vacations for July 1's. But whether you cross an ocean or merely Ocean Boulevard to get there, you'll probably take the time to visit the galleries, museums, churches, and libraries that tell the story of a place's past.

Music plays a big part in the life of many July 1's, and they may wander far afield to find it. Browsing through used albums for the perfect old blues number or sitting in the best box at the opera can be heaven to you; an all-night, after-hours jam session may feed your soul for weeks!

Antiquing is a pastime that many July 1's adore because it combines fascination with the past with the kick of finding a good buy. You may have a reputation as a first-rate bargainer, and those flea-market vendors might cringe every time they see your eyes seize on some dusty, musty treasure in their booths!

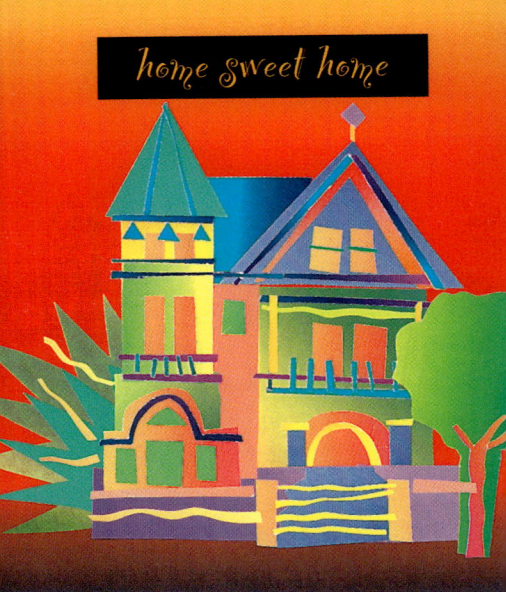

An old slipcovered sofa may seem merely worn and rumpled to some, but July I's will likely see it as cozy and inviting! Where better to settle down on a rainy afternoon for a soothing catnap? Comfort is incredibly important to most July I's.

July Is' many and various moods are reflected in their homes. Natural fabrics and earth tones might create a warm and comforting feeling in some rooms, but others are cool, smooth, and reflective. You could have a riotously colorful playroom next to a quietly furnished and formal living room.

Because cooking and eating are so extraordinarily gratifying to so many July 1's, having a comfortable and functional kitchen will probably be a must. But whatever room (or mood) you're in, you've learned that candles and low lighting can enhance both your surroundings *and* your sense of well-being.

Music, too, is key, so many July 1's will probably invest some of their closely guarded cash on a top-of-the-line sound system. And you will display your legendary music collection with pride. Not *everyone* can claim to have nineteen different recordings of Beethoven's Ninth as well as the latest from Nine Inch Nails!

And given your fondness for new movies and old classics, you also may have quite an impressive home theater setup. That way, you're always ready to invite the gang over for a marathon evening of pizza or popcorn, *Citizen Kane* or *Men in Black!*

how do you love?

Because July 1's are usually good at listening, they tend to be good at loving as well. After all, who doesn't yearn for a sweetheart willing to hear every story, gripe, and bright idea?

But the fact that July 1's can have trouble opening up may make a relationship one-sided. Don't fool yourself into thinking you're being coy and mysterious: Love is lots sweeter when you're able to communicate honestly and fully!

Many July 1's feel most comfortable with those who take life fairly easy and like to have a good time. The last thing you need is some wet blanket putting a damper on your fun! Likewise, a jealous lover is probably not the best choice for July I's. Your (usually) innocent yet high-spirited flirtatiousness will only ruffle his or her feathers!

When July I's fall in love, they may bend—if not altogether *break!*—their usually cautious spending rules. Buying that fancy box of chocolates, that wonderful silk tie, or that fabulous little painting your sweetie has been eyeing could be a temptation you find too hard to resist!

Given their unpredictable temperament, most July 1's would do well to seek a special someone who's stable and patient. Your true love should be able to understand when you're "thinking out loud"—and not *actually* changing your mind every two seconds! When you hitch up with your ideal mate, the prospect of lifetime happiness will convince you that you've made the perfect choice!

whom do you love?

July 1's (Cancer) get along best with:

Taurus (April 22–May 21)
Leo (July 24–August 23)
Virgo (August 24–September 23)
Scorpio (October 24–November 22)
Capricorn
    (December 22–January 20)
Pisces (February 20–March 20)

July 1's (Cancer) get along better without:

Aries (March 21–April 20)
Gemini (May 22–June 21)
Cancer (June 22–July 23)
Libra (September 24–October 23)
Sagittarius
    (November 23–December 21)
Aquarius (January 21–February 19)

July 1's seek out people who are:

sensual, steady, openhearted, sensitive, romantic, and committed.

July 1's avoid people who are:

aggressive, cerebral, detached, extravagant, brusque, or aloof.

famous/infamous people born today

Carl Lewis (1961) Olympic track-and-field athlete

Charles Laughton (1899) actor, *The Private Life of Henry VIII*

Diana (1961) princess of Wales

Leslie Caron (1931) actress, *Gigi*

Sydney Pollack (1934) film director, *The Way We Were, Tootsie*

Deborah Harry (1945) singer, Blondie, "Heart of Glass"

Jamie Farr (1934) actor, M*A*S*H

Fred Schneider (1951) singer, the B-52's,
    "Love Shack"

Twyla Tharp (1942) dancer and
    choreographer

Estée Lauder (1908) cofounder, Estée
    Lauder cosmetics company

Dan Aykroyd (1952) comedian and
    actor, *Saturday Night Live*

Willie Dixon (1915) blues bassist,
    "I'm Your Hoochie Coochie Man"

Pamela Anderson (1967) actress, *Baywatch*

Genevieve Bujold (1942) actress,
    Choose Me

oh what a day it was

JULY 1

First adhesive postage stamps are sold, bearing the likeness of Benjamin Franklin and George Washington, costing five and ten cents each (1847)

Annette Kellerman performs the first movie nude scene, for the film *Daughter of the Gods* (1915)

U.S. Post Office introduces the five-digit zip code (1963)

flashback: your past lives

In any past life, July 1's would have been in close connection to the water —or its symbolic equivalent, the world of the emotions. It is not unlikely that your past lives included the following occupations:

Submarine captain
Polar explorer
Amazon guide
Ice fisher
Oyster farmer
Professional surfer

your personal proverb

A good conscience makes a joyful countenance.

German proverb

a word of advice

Your leaning toward total comfort can sometimes lead to unsightly problems! Don't let yourself fall into slipshod habits just because they're both cozy and convenient! Beat-up sneakers, baggy sweats, and faded T-shirts may be fine around the house, but when you head out into the world at large you'll want to put your best foot forward!

looking ahead

Right now might be a great time to get involved in something that will offer satisfaction for years to come. Maybe you'll join a community choir or take a music appreciation class. Perhaps you'll volunteer to prepare or deliver meals for the elderly. Whatever you choose will likely help you fulfill your desire to make a real difference!